Proper Care & Feeding of a Huntin' Buddy

Humor, with a Little Huntin' Thrown In

Volume 1

BOB BALDWIN

JAY LEDBETTER

Published by Richter Publishing LLC
www.richterpublishing.com

Editors: Monica San Nicolas, Natalie Meyer & Margarita Martinez

Cover Artwork: Roger Luzardo

Inside Artwork: Rachael Albanito

Copyright © 2018 Bob Baldwin & Jay Ledbetter

All rights reserved. No part of this book may be reproduced in any form by any electronic or mechanical means (including photocopying, recording or information storage and retrieval) without permission in writing from the author or publisher. If you wish to purchase bulk or wholesale copies for libraries or book stores, please contact the publisher at richterpubllshiny@icloud.com.

ISBN: 1945812397
ISBN-13: 9781945812392

DISCLAIMER

This book is designed to provide information on hunting only. This information is provided and sold with the knowledge that the publisher and author do not offer any legal or medical advice. In the case of a need for any such expertise, consult with the appropriate professional. This book does not contain all information available on the subject. This book has not been created to be specific to any individual's or organization's situation or needs. Every effort has been made to make this book as accurate as possible. However, there may be typographical and/ or content errors. Therefore, this book should serve only as a general guide and not as the ultimate source of subject information. This book contains information that might be dated and is intended only to educate and entertain. The author and publisher shall have no liability or responsibility to any person or entity regarding any loss or damage incurred, or alleged to have incurred, directly or indirectly, by the information contained in this book. You hereby agree to be bound by this disclaimer or you may return this book within the guarantee time period for a full refund. In the interest of full disclosure, this book contains affiliate links that might pay the author or publisher a commission upon any purchase from the company. While the author and publisher take no responsibility for the business practices of these companies and or the performance of any product or service, the author or publisher has used the product or service and makes a recommendation in good faith based on that experience. All characters appearing in this work are fictitious. Any resemblance to real persons, living or dead, is purely coincidental. The thoughts and opinions in this book are that of the authors and not the publisher.

DEDICATION

We dedicate this book to the Almighty God, without Whom nothing at all can happen.

CONTENTS

Acknowledgments 2

Introduction 4

Bear-Initiated Spontaneous Science 7

Camp Nutrition 15

Things That Go GRRR in the Night 27

The Log Ride 35

The Proper Care and Feeding of a Huntin' Buddy Part One 51

The Proper Care and Feeding of a Huntin' Buddy Part Two 69

About the Authors 90

ACKNOWLEDGMENTS

Without the influence of Patrick McManus, *The Proper Care and Feeding of a Huntin' Buddy* would never have been written. Bob and Jay have never met Pat, and I'm sure that Pat (being a sensible man) would deny any connection with them! But it all began when Bob and Jay would sit around every night after a hunt and read Pat's stories. Pat's style of humor became seeds embedded in their fertile heads, and grew into what you see today.

Fueled by many cups of Earl Grey tea and hours of unsuccessfully chasing game all over North America, Bob and Jay have continued the McManus tradition of humor, with a little hunting thrown in for good measure.

Highest thanks that can be expressed go to Denise, Jay's bride of 39 years, and Shirley, Bob's bride of some 47 years. Not only have these fine ladies put up with weeks at a time when their husbands were away doing "research" for these stories, but they also were the first hearers (and editors) of the early versions of these stories. They are each to be praised for steadfastly pretending that they really did like their husband's huntin' buddy. Without their undying support and forbearance, these stories would not exist. Looking back on it, maybe the time away that Bob and Jay spent together gave these ladies a needed respite from all the story-telling that they endured once the men came home.

To those who have read our stories, expressing approval and insisting that we publish them, we thank you. Oh, and the check is in the mail. The end result of all this is that other unsuspecting hunters and fishermen will read, laugh, and repeat.

We would like to recognize Lindsay Dallison, an amazing artist, who crafted the cover.

And last but not least, we have to thank Richter Publishing for their encouragement, putting up with our editing faux pas and doing the legwork to make this work possible.

INTRODUCTION

The Proper Care and Feeding of a Huntin' Buddy is Bob and Jay's first book of hunting and fishing stories. The last two stories, which give the book its title, were birthed during Bob and Jay's first elk hunting trip together. The tragic series of events have been forever burned into the pages of their memories, so we figured it might as well be burned into yours, too—although you hopefully will not need as much immediate medical attention by merely reading these stories. You can thank us later.

Bob and Jay will both offer sworn testimony that their particular recollection of the events found in the pages of this book is pure, and that the accounts are written with a fastidious adherence to the truth, and nothing but the truth. But, of course, some bystanders might disagree...if they have by now recovered their powers of speech.

Bob and Jay met by phone back in 2002, and they really hit it off. Bob, not really knowing Jay (because of only having spoken by phone) made the mistake of accepting Jay's invitation to join him on a Colorado elk hunt. At the end of each fruitless day of elk hunting, Bob and Jay would have a home-cooked campfire dinner and take turns reading the hilarious stories of Patrick McManus. They always found themselves rolling on the floor, tears streaming from their eyes. Once they recovered, they would then continue reading the McManus stories, but would pop a few Tums. And this continued to be their pattern for many years.

After having read every story in every McManus book multiple times, Jay chortled that, "Hey, some of the things you do while we're hunting are nearly as funny as those stories. Maybe I should just make a few cursory notes." Bob enthusiastically agreed, "Well ... I guess ... if ... you must." Bob had no idea what he'd started. "The rest is history," as they say.

Laugh along with Bob and Jay, as they invite you into the wilds of northern Canada, the snowy slopes of the great Rocky Mountains, and deep into the deer woods of Texas.

Bob and Jay swear that the events you will read now could not be made up—they just happened—just like that. You will likely find some of your more funny experiences in this book, too. We know you will enjoy reading of their exploits much more than they "enjoyed" living them.

Neither Bob nor Jay have yet figured out how to graciously refuse an invitation to a hunting or fishing trip with one another, so they are even now still enduring endless days each year together. So, look for the next book in the series.

Good huntin' and good huntin' buddies.

BEAR-INITIATED SPONTANEOUS SCIENCE

Jay

Bob and I normally hunt in the beautiful mountains of Colorado, but on occasion, the trout streams that cascade out of the mountains beckon us to drop a fly or two at the heads of some of those inviting pools. And sometimes, when the hunting is not so good, we'll just spend the day fishing.

On a section of the mountain we call the "Backside," a particularly inviting section of Bill's Creek occupies the bottom of a huge crack in the face of the earth, with sheer cliffs rising 500 feet on both sides of a valley floor only about a quarter mile across.

We fish all the way to the far end of this segment, where the creek rushes through a very narrow crack in solid rock, cut by the water released by a huge glacier that previously occupied that valley. We call that narrow channel—over 20 feet deep, and only 10 feet wide—"The Slot." When the flow in the creek is robust, getting through "The Slot" is the final challenge of a very difficult, but very rewarding, fishing trip.

After surviving the harrowing wade through The Slot, we are rewarded with the gentler slopes of the upper canyon, and a climbable gradient. We climb to the road, walk back to where we parked the truck, and head back to camp to cook some nice trout for dinner.

The backside is almost never fished by the "easy water" fishermen of the area. Once in the valley, you're confined to the creek bed for the duration. Most fishermen find the almost claustrophobic nature of this canyon just too foreboding. But Bob and I are never deterred by extreme difficulty, and only rarely by impossibility.

And so it was on one fall day, when the bear hunting was as bad as we'd ever seen it, that Bob and I decided we'd fish the Backside. With visions of several past years of successes, we drove to the trailhead and rigged up. We then walked briskly for better than an hour to get to the confluence at the lower end of the canyon, where we stepped into the icy, unfished waters of this particular section of Bill's Creek. Soon, Bob and I were knee-deep in ice water, and busily stripping line out of our reels for our first casts.

Bob is the one who thoughtfully developed a strategy for fishing the backside, focused on keeping us both alive. First, we would never lose sight of one another as we fished up the creek. That's because we occasionally come across bear signs, in the form of scratched-up trees and bear poop. We would examine each pile of bear poop for such things as dog tags, little bells, and fishing reels. Bob insisted that I sniff each pile to see if there was bear-spray residue. Bob's like that. He won't dominate all the fun stuff on fishing trips.

The day was sunny and bright, and the green of the pine was framed with the high sandstone cliffs and sparkling water. The water that day was fairly swift, and although it averaged knee-deep, we were challenged with every step. We didn't walk up this creek, we carefully placed each step, hoping it would lead to the next. Going was pretty slow, but we gently coaxed trout after fat trout into the net. It was a glorious day. Each minute, each hour was put away in my mental scrapbook of favorite days.

About halfway between the confluence and The Slot, we were both standing in the middle of the stream. Bob was upstream, maybe 40 feet away, expertly laying a fly just above a little pool to the right. I had just released a nice fish, and was watching his technique, with my fly rod in the crook of my left arm. The gentle breeze kept the mosquitoes away, and the sun made the water sparkle. The larger rocks divided the fast water and made it chuckle and gurgle quite noisily in the passing. I was going to comment on this beauty to Bob, but the laughter of the stream would have dissolved my words before they reached him. So, I just privately took in the beauty of the scene and smiled.

That's when I noticed something different on the left bank, about 30 feet upstream from Bob, but out of his sight, as with singular intensity, he followed the drift of the fly through the little pool. What first caught my attention to this left-bank oddity was a combination of color—sort of blonde—and movement, headed right toward the creek. My mind quickly thumbed through the catalogue of things it could be, and after discarding all the more favorable (but impossible) entries, I was left with the only remaining option—it was a bear.

Focused on crossing the creek, the bear was moving quickly toward the water. It was no small bear, either. Bob was standing in the stream, his rod now across his arm, closely examining his artificial bug. He was still facing generally to the right, his back turned to the direction from where the bear was rapidly approaching. Bob's concentration on removing a wisp of moss from the hook in the Prince Nymph was complete. His head down, Bob had no chance of seeing what had just shocked me into full alert, this huge bear coming closer and closer to him, entering the creek a mere 30 feet upstream from where a perfectly calm Bob now stood.

The symphony of sound produced by the stream beating itself up against the larger rocks, coupled with the brisk flow of water gurgling past his legs midstream, dramatically reduced Bob's chances of hearing the bear padding across the grass and gently splashing into the edge of the creek behind him. This left Bob's hearing ability roughly equivalent to that demonstrated by a common patch of blueberries.

I would have thought that the sound my eyes made when slamming hard into the fully-open position might have caught his attention. Or maybe the stammered word "B-b-b ... b ... b-b" just doesn't penetrate the sounds of rustling leaves and churning water all that well. Either way, I just couldn't seem to find a way to catch Bob's attention with any sound that this bear couldn't hear much, much better.

Just as the big blonde bear splashed into the creek only a short cast upstream from Bob, he turned and looked up at me, flashing his characteristic broad smile. It was at about that time that I couldn't help but notice that the bear was so big, the knee-deep water barely reached its belly. I met Bob's smile with the look of mixed panic and despair that is normally observed on the faces of submariners two hours after being forced into a steady diet of X-Lax and spicy chili (with beans).

What Bob lacks in hearing, he makes up in visual acuity. His eyes quickly noticed my oscillating lower lip, and the tiny pointing movement of the pinky finger of my right hand. I was indicating with head movements, perceptible only to microbiologists, that there was something somewhat interesting "just there." These, together with subtle signs of hyperventilation, gave Bob several clues that maybe he should turn around and take a look. I recall that he was still smiling when he turned away from me.

By that time the bear was almost halfway across and just about directly upstream from where Bob was now turning to face the huge animal. In a nanosecond, every muscle in Bob's body fired at once. I do believe he levitated maybe a foot or so, and for a short while, he hung suspended above the surface of the water. Time slowed to a snail's pace. Poised there, in space, having left a pair of leg-shaped holes in the water, Bob used his keen intellect to improvise a solution to his obvious problem.

Much science springs from necessity, they say. Bob's whole-body jerk progressed immediately into a series of rapid movements of pretty much every part of his body, which initially seemed random, but quickly increased in speed to a point that requires a carefully calibrated oscilloscope to properly measure.

It was at that time that Bob, in a desperate attempt to disappear, went completely out of focus. Early in the whole process, he momentarily seemed to grow larger as his edges grew quite fuzzy, but very soon, all but a little bit of his center of mass had become pretty much transparent. For my part, I was able to grow a fairly convincing number of leaves.

While Bob was carrying on his interesting scientific experiment in levitation and invisibility, the bear crossed the stream in only two or three bounds and went right up the far bank and into the woods. As far as I could tell, the bear never looked to the right, nor paused in the slightest to see the odd tree downstream, and the ground-breaking scientific event happening close by. Oddly, bears never seem to be interested in scientific achievements.

As the bear disappeared, Bob settled back into the water, and the oscillations diminished to a low buzz. He turned toward me, a pronounced twitch still making one of his eyes strobe slightly off and on again. A wisp of smoke was rising from his hat. Trying to see if my eyes might ever close again, I was finally able to pry them out of the locked-open setting with a stem from one of the leaves I plucked from my arm.

Did we catch fish that day? I can't tell you. What was the rest of the trip like? Don't recall. But I do remember every vivid detail of a huge blonde bear crossing a stream on the Backside.

I still tell that story, but I don't do it with Bob around. Anytime he hears the word "bear" in the same sentence as "stream," the whole thing starts all over again for him. And besides, plucking leaves is painful.

>Good huntin' and good huntin' buddies.

PROPER CARE AND FEEDING OF A HUNTIN' BUDDY

CAMP NUTRITION

Bob

Learning the art of flying has great advantages. Since childhood, Jay and I have both looked skyward to see planes, big and small, course their ways across the blue expanses on trips we could only dream of.

Jay got his private pilot's license in high school, and even got a commercial license later on. I waited until a little later, but regardless of the timing, we both learned one essential aspect of flying ... weight and balance.

The long and short of it is that any aircraft must not be loaded too heavily, and the load must be arranged around a "balance point" of the aircraft so that it will fly. If the load is too heavy, it won't get off the ground, or it will barely fly. If the center of gravity of the loaded plane is too far forward or too far to the back, it will cause the plane to crash.

Both Jay and I carefully weigh our loads when we fly, and we position everything (including the people) in certain locations and seats to maintain that perfect weight and perfect balance.

Jay is a little more precise than most pilots in this endeavor, often asking his passenger to please throw away that candy wrapper or to dust off their shoes before boarding the plane. Jay has been known to carefully calculate the weight of the water on the plane after a rain, so as to include that in the mix. I have learned a lot from Jay when it comes to flying, because he's been at it a lot longer than I have, but I guess I've never quite gotten to the point of asking a passenger to spit out his gum before boarding, or including a "Did you get a haircut lately?" level of questioning.

Pilot training, along with years of calculating precise weight and balance for myriad different aircraft, also carries a severe disadvantage: the previous days of being a blissfully ignorant passenger in small aircraft are long gone. It is Jay's fastidious nature regarding flights in smaller aircraft that necessarily led to our latest culinary adventure in Canada.

Jay and I go bear hunting in Ontario each August, and the guide service flies us into a remote lake in a single-engine float plane. There we remain, just the two of us, isolated and alone, for about a week or 10 days, after which the pilot flies back into the lake, loads up our stuff, and takes us back home.

As part of the adventure, we also purchase fishing licenses so we can catch the nice-sized Northern Pike that inhabit the lake. It was those very fish that were to play a significant part in that year's food supply.

Rich, the bush pilot who flies us into the lake each year, is a wonderful guy with an easy smile. He's a seasoned pilot with untold hours spent in flying fishermen and hunters into remote lakes in Canada. He learned to fly back in the days when airports were mainly large, flat fields next to a town, and "navigation" was defined by most pilots as following railroads from one city to the next.

The plane Rich flies is just as old. It's a vintage De Havilland Beaver, outfitted with floats. Although manufactured in the 1940s, it remains the quintessential Canadian backcountry plane, with the characteristic deep-throated Pratt and Whitney radial engine. It's a workhorse, and will carry as much as a pickup truck.

But one thing about the trip always seems to nag at Jay. Rich never, ever seems concerned about how much our gear actually weighs. The old pilot mostly worries about the volume it occupies in the back of the plane.

Although Jay has flown some larger 1940s radial-engine planes, he has never done the "weight and balance" on a Beaver with floats. So, the pattern of the crusty old bush pilot telling us "hand me that thing next" just seems to violate pretty much everything that Jay holds dear as a by-the-book pilot. When you look up the word "hypervigilance" in piloting books, you just might find a picture of Jay.

So, that's how it was this year, as Jay and I were packing for our next Canadian hunting trip. He was drowning in a sea of doubt and concern. With some vivid memories of last year causing him to slightly hyperventilate, Jay had resolved to take decisive action to lighten the aircraft's load. After all, Jay rationalized, a lighter load is less critical to balance issues.

Add to this yet another of Jay's character flaws. Jay prides himself on figuring precisely how much food we will need, and it seems that in years past we have always hauled some of it back out when returning from the remote cabin. This year, all these characteristics combined into the perfect storm.

As is our custom, on the day before arriving at the guide headquarters, we shopped for groceries to take with us. Jay abruptly stopped pushing the grocery cart before the list was even half completed, and he began carefully eyeing the contents of the already heavily-laden cart. I rounded the corner with an armful of items and found him there, pensively stroking his beard. I could see his mind doing endless calculations as it always does.

Jay then turned to me and said, "You know, Bob. We took way too much food in last year. And I know that Rich doesn't weigh our supplies as he puts 'em in the plane."

"Yeah? And ..." I responded as Jay continued.

"Yeah, and that bit about barely getting off the water, and then jumping the plane up just as we got to the end of the lake," Jay was now using his hands to illustrate, "and barely clearing those trees was a little hard on my underwear."

I have no idea what I must have been thinking when I replied, "Wasn't that the truth!"

Looking back, I should have immediately clarified that Jay was right about the "jumping up at the end of the lake" part, and not right about the "too much food" part.

Jay immediately took my response as an affirmation regarding the weight issues, then started taking things out of the shopping cart. Out came almost all the canned chili, as well as a frighteningly large number of cans of lovely looking dinner-sized portions of stew.

"We'll catch all the fish we can eat," he said, happily restocking the grocery shelves. "Fish were just jumping into the boat last year." The perfect storm was beginning to form.

Memories are undisciplined. In spite of being ordered to remain in place, they seem to come and go as they please. In this case, many of Jay's memories had left, but most of mine had remained. In fact, as I now recall, during one day's fishing on that same lake last year, I had to haul Jay back into the boat after the only fish we'd caught all week squirmed out of his hands and slid over the side of the boat into the water.

Jay had lost his balance posing for a picture, and made the unfortunate choice to grab for the gunwale, thus releasing a secure grasp on the fish. Still, he did try to recover from his faux pas. I recall that he was screaming something about not letting it get away, but the end of the sentence was terribly garbled. That was the case because Jay was already waist-deep in the water ... in an inverted position.

Fishing memories are a special category of the larger universe of memories in general, ones which always seem to change with the passage of time. The mind is a fine distillery of fishing memories. The pesky realities of the events and their difficulties are left in the dregs. The inconvenient parts, left unused and unattended on dusty mental shelves, are disposed of in the mind's unnoticed garage sales. Their space is then taken up by the fine rendering of numerous big fish, easy catching, no sunburns, and only gentle, cooling breezes. Fine, aged memories are pleasing, but they totally lack nutritional value.

And so it was that year, as we packed about half the food we would normally take, about two-thirds the clothing, and even less niceties, such as toilet paper. Until I had met Jay, I had never calculated the weight of a roll of toilet paper and certainly never balanced its weight against its usefulness, a consideration I was soon to regret.

As we unloaded the pickup onto the dock at the outfitter's base in Ontario, we were pleased. Not only was the volume of the assembled gear significantly less than last year, but the weight was as well. Jay, in his inimitable manner, commented about how he and I had both lost better than 20 pounds off our personal frames since last trip. Jay had even gotten a fresh haircut. Everything seemed to be looking up. But the perfect storm was gathering power.

Rich, as was his usual form, stood on the floats of the Beaver floatplane at dockside, sized up the load, and began pointing to items on the dock saying, "Give me that now." He then piled and shoved what we handed him into the cargo area behind the second row of seats.

With his characteristic enthusiasm, Rich closed the doors, cast off the ropes, and the large radial engine coughed to life. With a gentle push of the rudder, the big yellow plane slid away from the dock and turned toward the open part of the lake. Rich turned and gave us his characteristic smile which said "everything will be just fine."

Jay looked out the window at the floats, and his eyes told me he was thinking "Boy, we sure are riding low in the water." I could see him mentally calculating the weight of the water on the floats to add to the accumulated load. He forced a smile, but it was the smile I often see when drivers in front of us do stupid things in traffic and feel compelled to just wave and smile, as if that makes it all better. I smiled and waved back.

Rich turned the plane into the wind, and the big radial engine began to roar, responding to the advancing throttle. As we picked up speed, we could feel the lake beginning to loosen its grip on the plane. The wings eventually gathered enough air to fly, and the floats finally cleared water by a foot or two. Rich pitched the nose downward to keep the plane just above the water, that way it would gather speed more quickly. He was clearly trading speed for altitude. Both Jay and I were wishing Rich would make the trade in the other direction. The wall of tall pine trees at the end of the lake was approaching quickly, and I saw Jay again doing mental calculations, this time regarding how much pine trees grow in a year, as we drew to within a few hundred yards of the trees.

At the last second, Rich jerked back on the control yoke, and the big plane lurched upward, clearing the trees by only a couple of feet. Both Jay and I involuntarily lifted our feet off the floor as the tops of the shoreline trees flashed just below the floats.

Jay, still holding his breath, turned and gave me a signal. He held up two fingers. No, it was not the sign for "victory." Neither was it the sign for "peace." Nor was it the number of feet by which the plane had cleared the trees, although that appeared to be a pretty good estimate from my position. I know Jay. He was letting me know that we have only two years of tree growth remaining until we need to lighten the load even further.

The flight to the remote lake was uneventful, and even enjoyable. The countless finger lakes of that part of Ontario passed below, as did the rugged scraggy hills that separated them. Here, the only thing that keeps Rich from flying is bad weather. And at this time of year, the season is changing toward winter, and low clouds and storms often will prevent him from taking hunters into, or out of, their remote camps. Last year, bad weather delayed our trip out to the lake. Predictably, that was one of those long dusted off and sold memories.

Soon, the gear was unloaded at the dock on the remote lake, and Jay and I saw Rich throttle-up the Beaver to leave. It was riding high on the floats, and jumped off the water in no time. As it turned away, we could see Rich's characteristic smile and wave, telling us, "Everything will be just fine." As the throaty roar of the radial engine faded into the distance, and as we took in the sights, sounds, and smells of our remote camp, we had to agree with Rich's assessment. We joyfully packed the gear up the short slope to the rustic cabin where we would spend a week of fishing, hunting, and wonderful fellowship.

The next few days were filled with wonderful pleasures. We slept late, ate breakfast, went fishing, then went hunting in the middle of the afternoon, staying on our stands until dark. It was a sportsman's dream.

Jay is our camp cook, and he prides himself on preparing carefully crafted menus for each day. The food is rationed, and he's careful to be sure we have enough for every day. On this trip, Jay had envisioned that days of successful fishing would fill out almost every evening's menu.

But the fishing proved quite difficult. We got sunburned. High winds kept us off the lake. Rainstorms brought deluges of such a volume that we lost sight of the nearby shorelines. Fish broke our lines and took our lures. We were down to our last steel leaders and last couple of spoons by midweek, and had very few fish to show for the effort. Yes, we had caught enough to make a meal, but only just barely. Jay had been forced to use our "emergency rations" (two cans of chili) early on so as to provide a modest evening meal. We were skipping lunches to extend the food, but that just made things more difficult.

It seemed that we weren't the only ones who were hungry. Even the fish we caught had empty stomachs. As I cleaned the few fish we caught, flies descended upon the fish carcasses with a frenzy that indicated they had also gone a while without a decent meal.

Earlier in the week, during a time of plenty, Jay prepared his normal breakfast of fried eggs, hash browns, and toast. After a few seconds' inattention spent fending off the frantic attacks of a starving butterfly, two pieces of toast became somewhat, how shall we phrase it ... overdone.

Jay doesn't serve food that isn't up to his high standards, so he quickly and secretly dispatched those scorched pieces of toast into the trash. In doing so, he couldn't help noticing that one of them displayed a burn pattern which looked for all the world like a portrait of Abraham Lincoln.

The final days of the week brought no real improvement in the fishing, and the food pantry was now empty. During one of his fly-overs, Rich dropped us a note tied to a wrench, telling us bad weather was right upon us, and he would have to delay our return flight for one or two days. I read the note to Jay, since he was unable to open his eyes, having cleverly slowed the rapidly descending wrench with the crown of his head.

The perfect storm of starvation was now fully upon us. But with only six sheets of remaining toilet paper, it did seem that it all would work out evenly. We wouldn't be eating enough to need them.

I was starting to do a few calculations of my own. "C'mon," I said, "Would three more cans of chili have caused us to crash?" Jay shrugged a silent response as I chided, "After all, we cleared those trees by better than two feet!"

Jay later admitted that he was at this time already contemplating the possibility of creating a burrito of sorts by rolling a mixture of sugar, moss, and cracker crumbs into the last few sheets of toilet paper and then frying that up in the pan. For the next meal, he would make omelets of old paper plates soaked in some yellow-colored Crisco discovered high on the back of a dusty shelf, and add in the contents of a small can of unidentifiable orange-colored substance we'd found abandoned under one of the unused bunk beds in the cabin.

At our last real breakfast, I contemplated our final non-survival meal. Approximately half of an egg of unknown origin slumped into one side of the reused paper plate. Off to one side of the egg rested three hash brown shreds, each of different age, color, and consistency. But what grabbed my greatest attention was what appeared to be a miracle ... a single, glorious full piece of toast. The toast was somewhat overdone, but it was still toast. I picked it up with a smile.

"Hey, look at this," I commented as I examined it closely. "This sort of looks like Abraham Lin—"

"Eat!" Jay interrupted, without looking up from his plate which sported identical contents. "At least we're having a few minutes of sunshine this morning."

Just then, we heard the throaty roar of a radial engine on a De Havilland Beaver pass over the cabin as Rich dropped her down gently onto the lake's glassy surface.

Jay smiled and threw away the last of the used paper plates, along with a couple of rusty cans containing something yellow and green that he'd found on the upper shelves. "Let's get our gear down to the dock," Jay urged. He didn't have to ask twice.

As Rich turned into the wind, and pushed the throttle forward to begin the takeoff, Jay and I looked across the calm surface of the lake. Everywhere we looked, there were widening circles disturbing the glassy water—circles where lots of big fish were voraciously feeding.

In the end, 10 days of hard hunting hadn't produced a bear, we didn't catch all that many fish, we got sunburned, and storms and high winds blew us off the lake at least twice. All our lures were gone, and we had no dry socks at all.

No doubt about it. In a few years, we're going to have some great memories of that wonderful trip.

        Good huntin' and good huntin' buddies.

THINGS THAT GO GRRR IN THE NIGHT

Jay

Bob and I had been hunting for bear for a couple of days at Lost Dog Lake in Canada. There are no grizzly bears in that area, just blacks. There are a couple of ways you can tell whether there are black bears in the area, and not grizzlies. First, you look at the scat. With blacks, the scat is full of vegetable matter, berries, and the like. Black bear scat smells like, well... like poop. With grizzlies, the scat often has the reflection of little bells, and often smells of pepper spray.

When being chased by a bear, you climb a tree to get away. At that point, it's important to be able to know whether you're running from a black bear or a grizzly. The way you can tell the difference is that a black bear will climb the tree and kill you, and the grizzly will push the tree over and kill you. Bob and I have studied our bears.

We were flown in by Rich in his old De Haviland Beaver float plane to a base camp on the edge of the lake. From that base camp, we would boat to all the various bear baits that Rich had placed around the lake. These baits are large steel barrels, secured with chains to large trees, and filled with all sorts of things that bears like to eat. Some were fairly near the base camp, but others were maybe a ten- to fifteen-minute trip by boat. We would occasionally take two boats when we wanted to hunt stands that were far apart from one another, or maybe we would just take one boat and drop one of us off at a stand that was on the way to a further stand. The latter was what we did on that fateful day.

Bob dropped me off at a stand located about a half-mile up a narrow bay off the main lake, where a small stream trickles into the lake. We like to call that particular stand "Slippery Rocks." It got its name from the approach to the stand from the water's edge. Once you tie up the boat to a log on the water's edge, you must negotiate a field of angular rocks, some as small as a hat, and others as large as a trash can lid, all surrounded by water. These rocks, especially those at the shoreline, are coated with a thick layer of moss, which is nourished by being occasionally moistened by the wave action from the lake. This moss, when wet, has the friction coefficient of grease. I hear that NASA is experimenting with wet moss as a cheaper and more effective alternative to high-end lithium grease for the giant transporter at Cape Canaveral.

The first rock that protrudes out of the water an inch or so is about 10 feet from the tree line, and you can dismount the boat there. With enough light, you can step from slippery rock to slippery rock the 10 feet to the tree line, and then maneuver across more slippery rocks that form the shallow creek bed to the stand. Getting from the boat to the tree line, past the bait barrel, and then to the stand takes careful foot placement and good balance. But, on occasion, neither of these will be present in sufficient quantities to avoid the inevitable. On a good day, you do an unrehearsed spontaneous dance. On a bad day, you slip down altogether, placing part of your anatomy at high velocity upon a sharp rock, and a bad word comes into your mind. In either case, the gravitational pull of the earth roughly doubles at just the time that your boot begins to slip.

What made the ordeal of getting into this particular stand worthwhile for me was all the bear sign. The bait barrel had been beaten up by a large bear, and it had huge dents in the steel all the way around. The ground was torn up to a couple of inches deep surrounding the barrel, where the bears had been digging up the goodies. A plastic bucket left by a previous hunter had teeth marks in it with punctures four inches apart. And a tree where Rich had previously put some peanut butter to help bring in the bears for us had been thoroughly thrashed in an attempt to open it up to get more.

I saw claw marks as high as my head, with the four claw gouges three quarters of an inch across. A little mental math told me that there had been a giant black bear working that barrel. Bob and I agreed, after a short wrestling match, that I would be the one to hunt the stand that first night.

So, at three thirty in the afternoon on a bright, sunny day, Bob dropped me off at the shoreline. He turned the boat around and then gunned the motor as he continued to his own stand. He gave me a friendly wave—at least it looked like a wave—and I began the treacherous trek some 40 yards back into the woods to take my place on the stand. I arranged the bait barrel so that I would have the best chance of taking a shot, and settled into the stand.

Time passed by, but that giant black bear didn't. The failing light finally made the sights on my bow dim to the point that I was unwilling to attempt a shot, so I gathered all my stuff, and descended the ladder. I crossed past the bait barrel and reached the little stream in a few steps. Then came the very difficult exit from the woods to a place where I expected Bob to meet me with the boat. I worked my way carefully to about halfway past the tree line, and carefully stood on one of the larger big rocks that peeked above the water. There were maybe two or three other rocks I could see just ahead of me, which were alternating in and out of the water as the gentle waves splashed over them. It was brighter on the edge of the tree line, and a beautiful sunset fading in the west made me smile.

I could hear the high-pitched sound of the little outboard off in the distance. Bob had also finished his hunt and was on the way back to get me. I expected to soon see the boat turn the corner at the mouth of the bay and head toward me. A chilly breeze from the water swept past and made me shiver. I stood motionless, my pack on my back and my bow in my hand, watching the fading light and hoping that Bob would soon round that far corner.

Then, I heard a twig snap behind me, back in the woods maybe 40 yards past the tree line. Not a small twig, mind you. I estimated it to be something just over two inches across, and it sounded like a cannon shot. Every nerve in my body went to red alert, and I turned to look back into the woods. The sky was still carrying a rosy glow out by the lake where I was, but past the tree line, all I could see was a black abyss. And I knew that the giant bear was back in that blackness, lumbering toward the bait.

Turning back toward the lake, I saw Bob heading toward me in the small aluminum boat. The engine seemed to be running okay, but the progress it was making in getting that boat closer seemed to be diminishing.

I looked over my shoulder, back toward the location of the sound I had heard just a minute before. The woods were black as pitch. There was no way I would be able to see a black bear in black woods, but I knew he was there just the same. He had just waited for me to get down from the stand before coming to the bait. He was a smart one, this bear. Nonetheless, I really didn't like the idea of being at ground level with this monster bear. What's worse was that I was standing in the fading light—completely visible, silhouetted against the lake and sky—and trapped against the water. If this monster charged me, I would not have a chance.

Bob and the boat were getting closer, but not at a pace that was at all satisfactory. It seems that the need for a boat to come get you off the shoreline is inversely proportionate to the speed of the oncoming boat. The boat was maybe 50 yards from shore, and Bob slowed the engine to an idle. He couldn't see the shoreline since it was shrouded in the dense woods, which left it obscured. I took another quick glance over my shoulder to see the black tree line. I knew the giant bear was less than 30 yards away, doing some calculations about whether to keep fighting that bait barrel for the tidbits it would offer, or opt for the tasty bow hunter conveniently perched on the slippery rocks at the water's edge.

It was at that precise time that I heard it. I don't know exactly how to describe what I heard. But I can only relate it to other things, because I have never heard that sound before. It was a combination of a low "huff" and the piercing sound I expect a velociraptor might make just before it charged. Then I heard a crashing sound as this bear began running through the woods, accompanied by three more guttural "grrr-huff" sounds. The remainder of what happened that night is pretty hazy for me, so I should have Bob finish the story, because he had a pretty good view of what happened next.

*

Bob

I had dropped Jay off at the "Slippery Rocks" stand on the way to the stand I was going to hunt, somewhat further up the finger lake. The boat was running well that night; getting Jay out of the boat really improved its performance. I had enjoyed my hunt, though I can't say I enjoyed seeing any bears, because I didn't. No bears came in to my stand. I was hoping to have Jay tell me of his hunt, since he was hunting the only stand with any really fresh bear sign. Turning up into the long, narrow bay, I headed to where I knew the stand was at the far end.

I was almost to the shoreline, but had to slow down a little. The dark reflection of the tall trees at the shoreline blended with the dark trees themselves, and I couldn't see precisely how far ahead the shore might be. I didn't need to worry about striking the propeller on any rocks, because the shoreline dropped sharply away. But I did need to be careful of the large rocks that sat just at the waterline and extended maybe 10 feet from the tree line. We used those rocks as stepping stones to get to the shore on the way in and out of the stand. I didn't want to hit one of those.

As it turned out, I didn't need to worry, because soon Jay was going to come out to me. I was maybe 20 or 30 yards from the shoreline when Jay passed me, going the opposite direction. In the failing light, I couldn't tell whether those were little roostertails coming off his feet, or steam. Either way, Jay was a blur from the waist down, and he was heading toward me across the water, gaining speed all the way. Actually, he did slow down a little as he jumped the boat, but then he accelerated again on the far side. This all caught me by surprise, since I knew there weren't any stepping stones out this far, and the water there was well over 10 feet deep.

I turned the boat around and gave it full throttle so I could catch up with him. Soon, I pulled alongside, and with a single motion, he stepped over into the boat and took a seat. He crouched down low in the seat to reduce any wind resistance as we pulled further away from the shoreline.

Soon we were back at the base camp, and I was able to find a screwdriver long enough to loosen Jay's grip on the sides of the boat. After helping him inside and pouring him a cup of tea, he finally began to breathe normally, and finally told me of his encounter with the monster bear. After a few cups of tea, Jay pretty much returned to normal—well, as normal as Jay can be.

Jay told me he'd hunt the stand I was in today, and I could hunt where the big bear was coming. So, I said I would hunt Slippery Rocks tomorrow, and Jay could go to my stand. I wanted to hunt as far away from him as possible. Nothing personal, but I think the smell of burned moss hanging around Jay might put off a bear.

> Good huntin' and good huntin' buddies.

THE LOG RIDE

Jay

Amusement parks have always been a favorite place for me. I have spent endless hour on top of endless hour at some of the finest amusement parks in the west, much of that time spent talking with my wife Denice as we waited perpetually for the line to advance. I would juggle my small fanny pack, which held my camera and accessories, as I applied yet another coat of greasy white sunscreen to keep the back of my neck from going from rare to medium well. Or maybe I would just set all that on the ground so I could slather with both hands. Then, I would find entertainment in staring at the backs of a sea of heads in line ahead. There is no end to interesting hairstyles, especially among teenage boys.

Of course, our mindless conversation, or casual lathering-up in sunscreen, was occasionally interrupted by actually moving forward a step or two. But the line was so long, and the progress so little, that I normally lost sight early on of the goal of riding the attraction. I occasionally had to inquire of Denice, "What are we going to ride when we finally get there?" She would remind me with a smile. I never knew whether she was right, but any answer seems to satisfy when you're in the perma-line.

The theory of actually getting to the front of the line, where you are afforded a fleeting opportunity to ride the attraction, seems only a distant legend by the time we actually get there, so I am always surprised when the attendant motions for me to step forward and straps me into the seat.

Now actually on the roller coaster, and heading up the first long gear-driven climb to the first free fall, I always remember the fact that I've left my camera on the ground next to the opened bottle of sunscreen just at the head of the line. So, I spend the rest of my time on the ride craning my neck, trying to keep the camera pack in sight. When we fly past the picture booth at the end of the ride, I have a perfectly-focused picture of all of us in the seats, screaming with delight. Well, you can't really tell that I'm screaming, because the picture is always of the back of my head. I've seen the back of all the other riders' heads, and they may as well see the back of mine for a while.

Most thrill rides at the parks have names like the "Mind Eraser," the "Hammer," or "Chaos." Those names are supposed to increase the fun of the ride by telegraphing the intensity of the experience through their names. But in my experience, such rides don't rival the fun of hunting, for hunting is an activity prone to surprise and excitement. And you almost never have to stand in line.

Bob and I love bear hunting, and we carve out a couple of weeks together each year to be certain that we can spend some time in the remote lakes of Ontario, hosted by Louis and Rich, the outfitters.

We're flown into the remote lake by the skills of Rich, as he deftly drops the De Havilland Beaver gently onto one of the long finger lakes.

After unloading our gear, Rich starts up the powerful radial motor, the throttle is pushed forward, and the big yellow plane disappears into Canada's clear blue skies. Bob and I are now on our own for the duration of the trip. After the low growl of the Beaver's engine fades, Bob and I lug our belongings from the short dock to the cabin where we expect to spend a week of pure joy.

The cabin where we stay is on one of the finger lakes. Each lake is very long—maybe two or three miles, but only 100 yards to a half-mile wide. All are connected end-to-end by smaller necks where the river gushes from one, to the other, to the next. Each finger lake is as straight as an arrow, giving Rich plenty of room to land the heavily-laden Beaver, and to get us to and from the cabin.

The finger lakes have been there a very long time, as have the dense forests on each side. The shallow lakes are occasionally littered with fallen trees, some of which have become waterlogged, and now rest on the shallow bottom. Other fallen trees rest along the shoreline, and are occasionally washed into the open areas of the lakes by wave action. So, one must be careful when boating on those lakes to avoid them.

Our daily routine is predictable. After breakfast, Bob and I cruise the lakes fishing for Northern Pike. After returning to the cabin at noon, we clean the fish, then take a one- or two-hour nap to be ready for the afternoon hunt. After arising, we dress for hunting and take the lone boat to the bear hunting stands.

Because we only have one boat, the one with the furthest stand will drop the other one off at his stand, and then take the boat to a location not too far from the far stand, where we stash the boat.

At dusk, we reverse the whole process. After retrieving the nearer hunter, we motor back to the cabin just as night is falling. The ride back is always beautiful. The little motor thrums in happy monotone as we slide over the stillness with a rising moon's reflection dancing between the heavily timbered high cliffs framing the corridor of shining black water.

Although there are several stands available just off the shoreline, there's one that both Bob and I both consider our far-and-away favorite. We call it "The Point." There, a tree stand is firmly secured to the trunk of a stately pine tree, about 25 feet up. This pine is one of several large trees located almost at the water's edge, well over to one side of a narrow point of land protruding into the finger lake. The limbs of the tree provide excellent climbing to the platform above. A bait barrel sits only 20 yards away from that tree, in a small clearing toward the middle of the point.

The location of the tree stand and the barrel give the hunter a decided advantage. The bear can only approach the bait from one direction—where the spit of land begins. With water on three sides, the bear cannot circle the tree and wind you. The prevailing winds always blow from the land to the tree stand, or across the point toward the tree stand. It's a perfect hunting set-up.

We get to this stand by easing the boat along the side of the point and beaching it gently underneath the big tree. From there, the hunter scrambles up the bank, circles to the other side of the tree, then climbs to the stand without any commotion.

Conditions here are perfect, and many very large bears are known to come to this barrel every week.

I shot a nice bear at this location last year, and saw maybe four more, so Bob really wants to hunt this particular blind this year. Last year, he reported he heard several bears in the brush around the stand that he occupied, but never got to draw his bow. I think he was just telling me that because he didn't want to shoot a much larger bear himself and show me up.

Each year, Bob and I devise several methods by which we determine which one of us will be able to hunt from "The Point." Each year, that method changes. The first year, we just made a gentlemen's agreement. That technique seemed prone to early failure, as neither Bob nor I are gentlemen. Besides which, I got to hunt "The Point" and he didn't.

The next year, we tried wrestling. But that method left us both out of breath, and so sore in the back that neither one of us could comfortably sit at the table, never mind sit in the stand.

We then tried a method by which one of us got up earlier from the midday nap than the other. In this case, the early-riser was able to avoid inconvenience to the sleeper by gently easing the boat well out into the lake before starting the engine, being careful to allow the other to sleep undisturbed. This kind of courtesy is common during our hunting trips. I didn't like that method nearly so much because I kept falling asleep on the stand, and Bob disliked it because he kept losing his voice from so much yelling.

I finished unpacking and made my room in the cabin my temporary home. I took a seat at the kitchen table. Bob apparently was more fastidious than I, since he lingered in his room a little longer.

I like to keep my mind active, so I filled the time with some calculations while I waited for Bob to finish whatever he was doing in his room, hunched over on the small wooden stool by the side of his bed. This time, just for entertainment, I was calculating how many seconds it might take for Bob to pull up his trousers and run from the outhouse to the shoreline when I was interrupted by his cheerful voice echoing from his room, "I have an idea on how we can choose who gets to hunt 'The Point' this year."

I smiled as I unwrapped the last of the handful of the Ex-Lax chocolates I brought along in my pack, dropping it into the saucer in my lap alongside the eight or nine already there. I slipped the wrappers into my pocket.

Bob strode briskly into the kitchen and pulled back a chair to take a seat. "Here, have a piece of chocolate," I said, as I raised the dish to table level. "You've been working hard in your room, all hunched over in there."

"Don't mind if I do," said Bob with a smile, as he plopped one of the chocolates into his mouth, and continued, "I propose that this year, we use a pair of dice."

"Dice?" I questioned.

"Yep, dice," he explained, "haven't you ever heard of 'casting lots'? They have been used for centuries to determine the will of God, so this method is quite biblical. The way I figure it," he said, "I think it makes sense that we just let God make the decision, and we both abide by it."

I leaned back in my chair, stroking my beard as I considered his offer. It had several attractive features.

"These chocolates are pretty good," said Bob, "can I have

another one?"

"Sure," I offered, "but don't get greedy; we need to make them last all week."

Bob popped another one into his mouth. "So," he continued, "if I throw snake eyes on the first try, I get to hunt 'The Point' this year," Bob offered, "otherwise, you can have it again." He leaned back in his chair to allow his offer to sink in.

Now, to be sure, I am not a person given over to gambling. I can't say that I've even held a pair of dice in my hands, so I don't really know much about how dice really work. But I do know some of the rudiments of probability. There are six faces to any cube. I know that "snake eyes" means that only one black dot will be visible on the top when the pair comes to rest, and I know that the chances of throwing only one "snake eye" will be one in six. So, by some rudimentary calculations, I determined that throwing two dice—both coming to rest with only the single black dot on top—would be far more remote. I was thinking that maybe Bob had, at best, a 1-in-36 chance of getting to hunt "The Point" this year.

Decent odds, I thought to myself. Besides, I was running out of other reasonable options, since Bob had started chaining the boat's fuel tank to his bed before lying down for his nap.

"Okay," I offered. "Throw the dice and let's see what you get." I did some additional mental math regarding how many days we would be hunting this time, then pulled the small plate containing the Ex-Lax back toward me, out of Bob's reach.

Bob stood up and pulled a pair of white dice from his shirt pocket, rattling them in his hand. A faint chemical odor was in the air. In a panic, I grabbed the plate of Ex-Lax and brought them casually past my nose. Nope, not them. Relieved, I set them aside, then stood and leaned over the table, looking directly down over the center so I could see the tops of the dice clearly. Bob threw them between us with a flourish, although he did accidentally knock off my glasses as his hand came up. Clearly, Bob isn't so good at dice, either. I retrieved my glasses from the table, and after putting them back on, took a look at the dice. Sure enough, beyond all odds, two black dots stared up at me like a cross-eyed snake.

"Well, who woulda thought!" Bob exclaimed as he leaned back and smiled with his hands on his hips. "God must be smilin' on me today!"

"Well," I responded, "God sure ain't smiling on the poor sap who made those dice, because neither one of those black dots is even near the center of …"

"Well, that doesn't matter a bit to me," Bob interrupted with a broad smile as he playfully pushed me back into standing position and scooped up the dice from the table, "snake eyes are snake eyes, right?"

I had to admit he was right. God had spoken, and who was I to contradict? "Well, let's load up our gear and get to the stands." I sighed, "I'll hunt the beach stand this week."

We soon had our bows and packs in the boat and were headed up the finger lakes to where I would drop him off at "The Point." I was in the stern of the boat, driving, since I would be at the furthest stand. The little fifteen-horse motor pushed the aluminum boat along nicely, and the vibrations of its power coursed into my hand as I gripped the rubber throttle/tiller that extended toward my seat at the rear. Bob was seated up front, scanning the lake ahead. Every now and again, he would extend his arm to the left or right, giving me steering directions so as to avoid the many shallows that can spell danger. Because the bow of the boat rides pretty high, even at full throttle, the front passenger can see much better than the one who steers. So, teamwork is important in taking the boat up these lakes.

Bob had taken the black nylon rope tied to the front eye of the boat and wrapped it around his wrist. We used that rope to tie up the boat, but it also served as a convenient stabilizer for the front passenger as well. Secured by that length of rope, one could even confidently stand up in the moving boat, since it offered a third point of stability.

Only a short distance up the finger lake from the cabin, we passed a floating log. It wasn't large, only 10 feet long and maybe a foot thick, and it was barely visible because only a half-inch or so of its bulk protruded above the water's surface. Bob signaled, and I saw the log just ahead off port bow. We needed to do something about that log now, while there was sufficient light to see. Later tonight, when we'd be heading back, it would be easy to miss it in the darkness. Running across it at speed would tear up both the boat and motors, and might even wake Bob. Yep, that log constituted a "hazard to navigation," as we maritime sailors know.

I yelled at Bob, "Let's deal with that log now!" He nodded and turned to face the log. I turn the grip on the motor to close the throttle, and we slowed to an idle. I pulled the tiller to the left, and the boat swung around, now at a right angle to the submerged log, floating only about 30 feet away.

Bob stood up in the bow, giving him a good view of the log. "Loop the rope around it and I'll pull it to shore," I yelled. Bob nodded, leaned over, and began using his free hand to gather the snarl of rope from beneath the gear in the front of the boat. Just then, the wake we had been making in the still waters of the lake caught up with us. The swells in the water began to rock the boat forcefully. I craned my head left and right to regain sight of the log, but I'd lost it.

Bob was still leaning over, working with the rope, blocking the remainder of my view of the now-hidden log. I really didn't want to run over the log and risk damaging the motor, so I stood in the rear of the boat in order to see. My feet were straddling the seat, and my hand was still on the tiller. The little motor was still in gear, and we were still approaching the log.

As I stood, another swell hit the boat. I leaned forward to regain my balance, pulling the engine with my hand a little off center. At that time, Bob felt the same imbalance, and he leaned back briskly, just in time to help the next swell rock the boat even further. I was using a balancing technique popularized by bull riders in the rodeo, with my feet moving forward and backward several inches in synchronous movement across the bottom of the boat, liberally lubricated by fish slime and motor oil. My left arm whirled around in a blur, describing a broad circle over my head. I suppose for the technique to work best, one must have a cowboy hat in that swinging arm, because it did little good for me.

As I lost my balance—convinced I was about to go over the edge of the boat—I grasped with my right hand, as best I could, the only part of the boat with which I had any meaningful connection—the throttle/tiller of the motor.

It became immediately apparent to me that my wild body movements were generating more instability than that one hand was able to correct. This was true, especially since my thumb was either unwilling or unable to successfully cooperate in the gripping process. My irresponsible thumb had independently slipped maybe an inch upward. That left my four remaining fingers in charge of the rest of the process, and they were each still fully convinced that the gripping-for-dear-life activity was by far the best course of action. Just as the tiller followed my body's next iteration of the slime-slide to the right side of the boat, the four cooperating fingers independently rotated the throttle to a higher setting ... a much higher setting.

It is at this point that most of what happened next became a blur. If I close my eyes, I can still see pretty much all of it in vivid detail, although I must admit that most of what I see with my mind's eye is in shades of blue, due to the very high speeds at which the events occurred.

As the boat accelerated briskly, in an incredibly tight left turn, I calmly regained my seat. The sudden application of my weight to that side of the boat made it lurch even further out of balance, aiding in the tightening turn and rocking the boat even further to its side. By now, Bob had recognized the futility of gathering more rope, and instinctively lurched into a fully upright position. Bob then took over the part of the rodeo cowboy. With impeccable timing, the boat launched off the next wake swell and rose well up into thin air, with only the propeller submerged. Unimpeded by the drag of water, the engine was able to increase its leverage. The rate of rotation increased exponentially, and a grand physics experiment was well underway.

Bob was still hanging onto the black rope with his left hand, which kept him in the standing position as he was then suspended weightless in space. Because of the weightlessness, his feet also lost traction on the slippery bottom of the boat. Bob instinctively began swinging his right arm wildly in a circle behind him. He calculated that possibly counteracting forces, created by the centripetal action of his swinging arm, might slow our rotation.

Bob looked back at me with a look that I immediately recognized. His expression said, "This would be working a lot better if I had a cowboy hat." I saw his mouth moving in slow motion, but no words ever reached me.

I say he looked "back," but I am not all that certain that he actually did. At that time, "back" started to lose meaning. The boat was rotating about its center axis at a rate that only nuclear physicists can understand. I think I recall seeing Bob three separate times during one of the rotations, and the last of those occasions was two weeks prior, while he was mowing the lawn. I do believe I also saw the back of my own head at least once, which I recognized immediately from countless photos in the theme parks of the west.

Thankfully, my right thumb finally decided that it made sense to rejoin the crew, and with its cooperation, I was able to rotate the throttle to the idle position while centering the tiller. The boat splashed down and came to rest in the center of a circle of hissing, foamy water, with the log positioned at 90 degrees to the boat, equally divided to either side, just in front of the motor's heavy transmission housing.

"Never mind, Bob, I've got it," I said calmly.

Bob didn't respond right away, although I think his lips were still moving from his last attempted statement.

I left the motor in gear and was able to ease the log carefully to the nearby shoreline with the help of the motor's downward transmission housing. After three failed attempts, Bob was finally able to sit down on his seat, the rope still quite tightly wound around his left wrist. His other arm finally rotated to a stop at his side. I think I smelled a faint odor of clothing smoke.

As we reached the shoreline, Bob turned and told me, "I really, *really* have to use the bathroom. Put me up on the shore, now!" That was pretty easy, once I got the log to the shoreline. Bob scrambled up onto the shoreline and disappeared into the woods with his hand on his behind. I sat back in the boat to relax. The aluminum of the boat seemed curiously warm to the touch.

As I waited for Bob to come back out of the woods, a revelation hit me. Bob was just using that "go to the bathroom" statement as an excuse to leave me in the boat alone, so he could walk back to the cabin. I was right, because Bob didn't come down from the dense woods for a very long time. He had won the right to hunt "The Point" fairly and squarely, but he really wanted me to hunt it instead. Bob knew that I would never hunt it against the will of God, so he had to do something to make it clear to me that I was to hunt it today instead.

Bob is so generous. He'll do that kind of stuff for you, and find a clever way to keep from letting you know that it's his plan all along. So, after yelling "Thank you" several times in the direction he disappeared, I boated down the lake to "The Point" to hunt.

On the way to "The Point," I saw a tiny bottle of white automotive touch-up paint rolling around in the bottom of the boat. Some other people must have accidentally left it in the boat before we arrived. I picked it up. Bob liked this kind of stuff. He really takes care of his pickup. I would give it to him in a couple of days, as a "thank you" for allowing me to hunt the best spot on the lakes today.

Bob has the highest regard for the skill I used to maneuver the boat deftly into a perfect position to move the log, without his assistance, and without even getting the rope wet. He keeps calling this whole episode "The Log Ride," as if it were some sort of amusement park attraction. I guess that's why hunting trips provide better fun than amusement parks. Fun times and surprises are around every corner.

Good huntin' and good huntin' buddies.

THE PROPER CARE AND FEEDING OF A HUNTIN' BUDDY
PART ONE

Jay

True huntin' buddies are hard to find. Oh, you can find a hunting *acquaintance*, or maybe even a hunting *companion*. But those relationships don't hold a candle to the depth possible with a true *huntin' buddy*.

A huntin' buddy will give you the last cookie in the box. A huntin' buddy will insist that you hunt the best stand. A huntin' buddy will hand you his last pair of dry socks. A true huntin' buddy will help Bob clean his animal after he made a kill, and even hold his knife and hat while he is throwing up behind that bush over there.

A true huntin' buddy will hold your shotgun or bow as you cross that waist-high barbed wire pasture fence. He will later protest that he was so completely focused on holding your hunting gear that he couldn't reasonably have been expected to see, much less warn, of the extreme hazard provided by that odd extra smooth wire running through insulators on the far side of that same fence.

This same huntin' buddy will just stand there, watching your quick series of desperate attempts to complete the botched half-crossing of that fence, as the electric fence controller fires another, then another, then another high-voltage charge through that smooth wire. Predictably, and against your will, the bolts of electricity will find your leg a convenient shortcut directly to ground.

That same huntin' buddy will devote full attention to the whole sequence of events so he can provide a clever series of comments regarding the amazing moves you just made—telling all your friends about how you quickly and expertly executed a number of very complicated gyrations combining what he will describe as "Olympic-style gymnastics with professional rodeo bull riding."

This huntin' buddy will help everyone remember this event year ... after year ... after year, and with every retelling, this huntin' buddy will add yet another embellishment to the narrative, supplying significant "details" that I am pretty sure *never actually happened*. Especially the part involving urine. Just for the record.

In summary, you can search your entire life for a *real* huntin' buddy, and if you find one, you should put considerable effort into keeping him. After years of carefully cultivating the relationship with your "huntin' buddy," you will not wish to endanger it with careless acts.

But really, the proper care and feeding of a huntin' buddy isn't "work." If you stop to consider the possibilities, there is no end to the things you can do to your huntin' buddy.

In my experience, there are a number of common offenses one might commit against a huntin' buddy. So, as a service to the hunting community, I will now pass along some of my best hints, and even some sage advice, on how you might best preserve this hard-won relationship.

For ease of understanding, I will first set the stage for each common offense by a summary statement. I will then offer a useful illustration in story form, set against the backdrop of an imaginary hunting trip to Colorado, in search of elk.

For lack of a more appropriate cast of characters (and not wishing to offend any innocent hunters out there whose names might coincidentally match those chosen here), I will simply cast Bob and myself in the parts of the "huntin' buddies" exemplified below.

Okay, so let's begin by setting the stage with some rudimentary facts regarding this "imaginary elk hunting excursion in Colorado" which will form the foundation of our illustrative scenarios.

Bob and I had been bowhunting for several days in early September, high in the Rocky Mountains of central Colorado.

The weather had been a little warmer than usual for this time of year, and although the aspens had long since turned golden and had dropped some of their leaves, the snowline was still well above 12,000 feet.

The unseasonable weather and lack of significant snowfall had allowed the elk to stay high on the mountain tops, well above the tree line. Coincidentally, this also put the elk well above the minimum-saturation-of-breathable-air-necessary-to-sustain-human-life-line as well.

An axiom of elk hunting is "hunt where the elk are." So, we left our comfortable camp trailer in the valley at a very early hour, parked the pickup at the highest dead-end road we could access, and began the steep climb in the predawn darkness. The difficult climb brought us to our target altitude just at the tree line by sunrise, but we were already winded and exhausted before beginning the hunt.

After resting for almost an hour to regain some of our stamina, and gathering some precious but meager warmth from the rising sun, we glassed the bare slopes for the elk herd, which was constantly on the move. Moving several times laterally across the terrain gained fresh vantage points, and we finally located the distant herd.

Sadly, the remaining usable hunting daylight gave us insufficient time to properly close to a reasonable stalking position. Each afternoon brought a long trip down to the camp. A short night's rest never quite allowed us to recoup our strength, so these hunts grew more and more difficult with every new day. Our nearest shot at a trophy bull this week had been in the neighborhood of 2,000 yards. Our hunting tactics were clearly not working.

One day we didn't have the stamina to make the morning climb, and we hunted low, near where we had been parking the pickup every morning. There was lots of elk sign, but it was all old.

As we ate our lunch from the tailgate of the parked pickup, we noticed something new. There was a brisk wind carrying gray clouds across the peaks from the northwest. They whispered to us that the weather was going to make a dramatic shift this evening. I predicted a light snow, which would drive the elk down into the darker timber where we could hunt them. Bob and I immediately resolved to make some dramatic changes in our hunting tactics as well, in hopes of changing our fortunes.

We purposed to abandon our lower camp (and the comforts of the camper trailer) in favor of setting up a tent at a "spike camp" in the highest flat spot we could find on that rugged mountain. That way we could sleep among the elk, preserve our strength, and extend the hunting day dramatically.

The problem we were facing now was a shortness of time. When we finally decided to take this important step, the sun was already on the decline. Even if we left immediately, we would likely finish the climb in the dark. We could see the first sprinkles of rain that normally precede snowfall leaving darker stringers below the clouds at the crest of the mountain. Soon this would change to snow. We didn't want to try to climb this mountain in a snowstorm. We had to get moving, and we had to get moving now.

With a high degree of urgency and anticipation, Bob and I threw camping gear and food for three days into our backpacks. We locked the truck, turned toward the naked peak, and started the climb. Although parked as high as the roads would allow, we still needed to gain almost 800 feet of altitude on a 40- to 50-degree incline. We were heavily loaded, but we would only have to do this once, rather than daily. And we'd be able to get two more hours of sleep and extend our hunts by an hour on the back end as well. It was a good plan. Nah, it was a *great* plan.

With these basic foundations laid for our imaginary hunting trip, we can continue with some illustrations of some things that in my imagination, perchance, might actually go wrong. For lack of a better word, I will just call each of them a "sin." At least that is what Bob, since that time, has always insisted on calling them.

Sin: Loading your huntin' buddy's backpack significantly heavier than yours.

Example: For the purposes of this illustration, let's imagine that for a considerable time, I was given sole responsibility for packing both Bob's backpack and mine. That was due to Bob's complete lack of advance planning, leaving him woefully behind in the process of getting his cold-weather hunting gear out and ready to pack.

I was much better organized than Bob, and had all my gear laid out. I would also like to point out that when one is packing in a hurry, with one eye on the darkening sky, it is just not possible to carefully weigh everything and do complicated math to be sure that each pack weighs the same.

And when your huntin' buddy is an "I've-got-better-hunting-stuff-than-you-do" kind of guy (and always brags that he has a bigger backpack with more external pockets), then maybe, *just maybe*, the larger volume of that pack (together with all the external storage pockets) lends itself to carrying a few ... mind you, only a *few* ... more things. And it's not *my* fault that the six-man tent I brought would only fit in Bob's pack.

Oh, and this brings me to one more helpful hint for hunters as they climb up the mountain to the spike camp with a huntin' buddy: When taking the first rest stop, *never ever put your pack next to his on the ground*. Your huntin' buddy will invariably want to move your pack over to some other place, let's say a couple of feet to the left ... for a better look at a patch of flowers or colorful aspen leaves where the packs were resting ... and then your huntin' buddy will involuntarily perform a comparison on the perceived weight differences between the two backpacks.

At such times, your huntin' buddy will invariably forget that verified truth memorialized by Crocket's Axiom: "Regardless of the true weight differential, the backpack of another companion will always seem lighter than your own." Regrettably, the conversations accompanying the remaining trip to the spike camp will be driven by the effects of another well-worn bromide: "First impressions are the longest-lasting."

Regardless of your attempts to correct him, your huntin' buddy will wrongfully (and continually) complain to you about the perceived differences in weight for the remainder of the climb, and will not listen to reason from that point forward.

So, I offer here another helpful hint: Since your pack is lighter … er … uh … *thought to be lighter*, this should give you a decided psychological advantage in climbing. Thus, you can maintain a pace that keeps your huntin' buddy in a somewhat "winded" condition. As he gasps for shreds of breathable air in your wake, he will be unable to clearly enunciate any of his incessant complaints.

It's important that you remember that your huntin' buddy really doesn't wish to damage your close relationship by making poorly-considered wrongful accusations. Because you know he's not thinking clearly due to the thin air, by taking this appropriate action, you are really doing him a great favor. You are helping him avoid the huntin' buddy sin known as "Constant complaining during a climb to establish a spike camp." He'll thank you later… or at least, he *should* thank you later. But don't hold your breath.

Sin: Laughing when your huntin' buddy takes a spontaneous rest break.

Example: During our imaginary climb, let's say after a couple of hours of climbing, both of us were growing quite tired. Bob and I were about halfway up the mountain, and beginning to cross an aspen grove, clinging precariously to the steep slope.

Bob and I rationalized that we would move more quickly through the aspens than through the dark timber to either side. The two-inch diameter trunks of more widely spaced aspens were easier to negotiate than a thick grove of blue spruce requiring lots of detours. The glistening layers of aspen leaves on the ground formed a tapestry of brilliant colors, and both Bob and I often paused to take photographs. Also, we expected the trunks of the aspens to offer occasional handholds for pulling ourselves up another step or two. Unfortunately, this now exhausted all the anticipated benefits of this route. But there were a number of hidden detriments—very important detriments—of which we were totally unaware.

In hindsight, I have an accurate analysis of the situation. Aspens grow in rich soils, and since aspens only sport a smattering of leaves and limbs concentrated at the upper reaches of the tree, sunlight easily reaches the ground. Lush mountain grasses take advantage of these conditions, and these dense grasses have all their thin blades bent downhill from the influence of falling snow and rain. Think of short, smooth dog hair.

Aspen leaves are rounded, flat, and shiny. When moisture is drawn between the layers of fallen leaves, the coefficient of friction drops to nearly zero.

So, when the slick mountain grass is covered with a few

layers of moistened aspen leaves, the footing becomes treacherous.

I was in the lead as we ascended, for two main reasons. The first was to have the first chance at any breathable air, and more importantly, to maintain a pace that kept Bob too winded to continue to complain.

About every tenth step upward, I would hear a sudden "swoosh-oof." I would then turn around to find Bob sitting (and sometimes reclining) on the wet leaves, slowly shaking his head and muttering to himself.

Helpful hint: When climbing to establish a spike camp, consider going *around* those aspen groves, staying in the thicker pines. The going will actually be quicker, and it won't provide your huntin' buddy a convenient excuse for taking a lot of rest breaks.

Now, to hear him tell the story today, Bob will protest that his ability to keep either of his feet under him would suddenly disappear. I can't help but think Bob was just making an excuse to take a quick series of rest breaks so he could catch his breath and begin complaining again.

Regardless, one should not comment on what one's huntin' buddy's doing by saying, "Are you taking *another* rest break, Bob? We're *never* going to get there at this pace. Har, har, har."

Sin: Not finding a sufficiently level place to put the tent.

Example: Daylight was quickly fading, and it was clear that Bob and I would need to find a place to set up our spike camp in a hurry. As we got pretty close to the tree line, I was well ahead of Bob, and began searching the thick timber for a reasonable spot to put the tent.

Let me begin by saying that it should be totally obvious to even a novice hunter that there won't be a lot of level places on the slopes of high mountains. The best anyone should be expected to do is to find the best flat spot, as close to level as possible.

It is important to note at this time that when one has been climbing very steep slopes for hours, any significant departure from vertical seems relatively level. Under these conditions, the sudden appearance of a gentler slope nestled there among stately pines, with good soil, relatively free of large rocks, looks as level and inviting as a neighborhood lawn.

On the other hand, Bob has in succeeding months repeatedly pointed out to me that "flat" is not an interchangeable term for "level" when searching for a tent site. When challenged as to why he didn't protest when I selected that particular spot, he just came up with the lame excuse that I had been "breathing up all the available oxygen" before he could get to it, and further that he was just "too winded to say anything." He would follow that by mumbling something about the pace we were keeping and such.

And let's continue to imagine that as I was packing the backpacks for this hypothetical climb to the tree line, I had the foresight to bring along some large tent spikes that I personally made to hold the tent in place, even in brisk winds. The spikes that come with these tents from the manufacturer are simply cheap flimsy aluminum rods bent over at the top. They are light, but won't tolerate being pounded through difficult soils, or around rocks.

Now, allow me a short departure from our main subject to give a helpful hint regarding making functional tent spikes. My homemade tent spikes are eight-inch "bridge nails" equipped with a large fender washer, which I slipped onto the spike and welded into position just below the head of the nail. Okay, these spikes are a *teeny bit* on the heavy side, but they make up for that by being really sturdy. And they won't bend when you pound them into place with a big hammer—or even a rock. They hold your tent securely on a significant slope, or even through a brisk wind. A true huntin' buddy will appreciate this nice touch. These important features make these sturdy spikes ideal for use in the "mountain spike camp" application.

Because I want these stakes handy for immediate use when unrolling the tent, I roll them up into the center of the tent as I put it away. Thus, they are securely stored for the next use, and you can't forget them. Bob didn't even know they were there until he unrolled the tent. And I hardly noticed the extra weight when I loaded the tent into Bob's backpack.

As I recall, after unrolling the tent, Bob immediately recognized their superior value. He just kept on gushing, "Thanks soooo much, Jay, for allowing me to carry those spikes up the mountain," he repeated over and over.

You are quite welcome, Bob. Really. Don't make such a big deal about it. Yes, they are really good tent spikes. It's just one of those subtle things that a true huntin' buddy thinks about in advance.

Fortunately, I had rolled one additional spike into the tent when putting it away months ago. That was to prove very useful.

The big dome tent was up in no time, and we oriented the door to face to the left as one viewed the tent from downslope. Now for another important spike camp hint: It is important to have the tent door facing *across* the slope, not downslope. An open door straight downhill might serve as an easy escape route for food, clothing, or gear to tumble to the lower edge of the tent in response to gravity. After easily breaching the short threshold, these items will quickly retrace your path back to the parked truck.

On a related note, I have discovered that camping and hunting gear both have an unnatural fear of altitude, and will take every opportunity to retreat to lower elevations. So, heed this warning and avoid the dilemma caused by a total lack of food in the camp, but still being able to clearly see the shiny glint of midday sunshine reflected by six glorious cans of delicious stew slumped against a big rock some 150 yards straight downhill from the tent. In such circumstances, someone might perchance say something like, "A true huntin' buddy would go down and get those cans of stew so that we can continue the hunt." But as a word to the wise ... don't do it! Because these rebellious food items will just take the first opportunity to go right down there again. Just sayin'.

Bob's pack proved too full to accommodate the large hammer that I had back in the pickup, so I graciously allowed Bob to use a large rock to pound in the tent stakes. As he was doing that, I carefully brought my gear inside (to help hold the tent in place as Bob did his work). A true huntin' buddy will provide this type of subtle assistance without drawing further attention to himself.

As I was stowing my gear, I noticed that the slick outer nylon shell of my sleeping bag wouldn't stay in place upon the slick nylon floor of the tent. I carefully arranged the bag, but it would immediately slide down into a wad at the lower margin of the tent. I reasoned that the problem was that it just needed more weight—which I could easily supply by being inside it—to stay in place. But for now, I just needed some meager assistance to hold my bag in place until bedtime.

As Bob hammered the spikes at one of the tent's corners, he carelessly allowed a tiny piece of finger to cushion the impact of the rock upon the spike. He later swore that this happened because as the hammering rock was on its way down for its first blow, someone in the tent suddenly pulled on the tent's floor, pulling that little cloth loop surrounding the loose stake an inch to one side, thus angling the big nail's head toward his fingers. Silly Bob ... such a funny guy ... there was nobody in the tent but me. Har har.

Regardless, Bob immediately began an impromptu dance. You know the one. Where one hand grasps the other, and both are placed securely between clenched thighs as one hops about in a random pattern (with or without the addition of a number of primitive guttural vocalizations).

At this time, I realized the serendipity of having an extra tent spike. I stepped outside as the arc of Bob's hop-dance took him to other side of a large spruce some 50 feet away. I found Bob's hammering rock unattended and used it inside the tent to drive the extra tent spike through a handy cloth loop at the very top of my sleeping bag, through the tent floor. With a couple of well-placed blows from the rock, the big nail disappeared to its full length into the soil. My bag would stay in an ideal location at the high end of the floor until I could occupy it, and I could easily repair the small hole in the tent floor back home in the off-season. I put my pack and hunting gear below my bag, at the low side of the tent, so that it wouldn't be in the way.

Being a good huntin' buddy myself, I then replaced Bob's rock where he had previously tossed it. He would recognize it as the correct rock from that prominent splotch of fresh blood. I then quietly retrieved Bob's pack and hunting gear (and after stepping back a little to allow Bob a clear path to hop-dance past the tent door as he completed his next pass through the camp) I re-entered the tent.

I unrolled his sleeping bag and put it into place a couple of feet further from the door than mine. Bob had thoughtfully purchased a sleeping bag with a rougher exterior, which did seem to stay in place on the tent floor without any further efforts. Both sleeping bags were oriented in the "head-high" position, which is essential for comfortable rest, especially following a full meal.

Since Bob's bag was less slippery, I was confident that the larger flat rock I'd put in the very top of the bag would keep it in place until Bob could get into the bag and secure it in place with his personal bulk. Then he would set the rock aside, providing a convenient resting place for his glasses. I knew that Bob would thank me for this extra touch later on.

Thinking ahead, as a good huntin' buddy does, I figured Bob might need something further from his backpack during the night. Since Bob was entering the outer-orbital phase of his hop-dance, I was unable to get his attention to inquire. So, I thoughtfully put the heavy pack within easy arm's reach, just above the top of his sleeping bag. I also pulled the Band-Aids out of one of the side pockets of his pack, and placed them where I was sure he could find them upon re-entry.

If you want to have a good huntin' buddy, you should work to be a good huntin' buddy. And I had been consistently "going the extra mile," as they say.

Bob zipped up the tent door just as sleet (that would soon turn to snow) began to pelt the tent. We wolfed down some snack foods for our evening meal, which I opened for Bob (since he was yet to regain full use of his left hand).

Soon we zipped into our bags, excited for the sounds of nearby bull bugles in the morning. Both Bob and I are experienced campers, so we folded up our coats and shoved them into the upper parts of our bags as expedient pillows.

In moments, I was asleep. But not for long. It seemed that at least twice I was awakened by Bob grumbling loudly and once again inch-worming his way upward out of the avalanche of our gear at the lowest margin of the tent.

In the morning, Bob reported he'd just finally given up trying to regain his initial sleeping location high in the tent's floor, and had just spent the rest of the night in a wad at the bottom of the tent, pinned there by his backpack across his chest.

He attributed his difficulty in rejoining me at the high side of the tent floor to what he described as an "unreasonably high slope angle at the camp site," which he emphasized was selected by me. He also attributed his inability to sleep even in the crowded hammock formed by the lower margin of the tent to the late discovery of a mysterious sharp, flat rock which had somehow found its way into his sleeping bag.

This reminds me of another helpful hint for hunters who are intent on preserving the valuable huntin' buddy relationship: You don't need to tell him *everything* you know. What your huntin' buddy doesn't know won't hurt him.

But do take the opportunity to pack his backpack with lots of salve and bandages, just in case he accidentally somehow spends most of the night with a big, sharp, flat rock in his sleeping bag. That way you can continue to be the best huntin' buddy of them all.

Good huntin' and good huntin' buddies.

PROPER CARE AND FEEDING OF A HUNTIN' BUDDY

THE PROPER CARE AND FEEDING OF A HUNTIN' BUDDY
PART TWO

Bob

Jay and I agree. True huntin' buddies are hard to find. You can easily find a hunting *acquaintance*, or maybe if you work harder, a hunting *companion*. But those relationships don't hold a candle to the joy that comes along with a true *huntin' buddy*.

I strive to be a good huntin' buddy. I have given Jay the last cookie in the box. I have occasionally insisted that he hunt the best stand. I've even given him my last pair of dry socks.

I'm sure Jay would do the same, if the circumstances ever presented themselves.

Jay really does try, though. He once tried to help me clean a deer I had just killed, but he suddenly had to run off into the woods to take a "rest break." Sadly, something out there in those woods made him terribly ill, and he was unable to come back to continue the work until I was essentially finished. Frankly, I am glad he was off in the woods. The sounds of his constant yacking were starting to get to me.

To Jay's credit as a huntin' buddy, he is always volunteering to lead the way, thus exposing himself first to whatever dangers might lie ahead. I recall one time in particular, when we were hunting quail. We had busted the covey in one brushy pasture, and they flushed into the adjoining pasture. We needed to hurry in order to keep them from regathering and outdistancing us.

We trotted to the waist-high barbed wire fence on the near side of that pasture. Arriving at that fence, Jay thrust his shotgun into my hand as he grasped the top wire and swung his leg upward. I stepped back to avoid being kicked by his ungainly technique. I tried to warn him that he might want to check that fence a little more closely, but he was already committed. "Aw, c'mon, Bob," he chided. "... you aren't scared of a little barbed wire pasture fen—bvd-bvd-bvd ..." It was about that time that I saw for the first time the source of Jay's sudden onset of poor enunciation.

Hidden on the far side of that fence was an inconspicuous smooth wire running through insulators suspended high upon the wooden fence posts. Before Jay could recover from the last jolt, and concentrate on freeing his clothing from the barbed wire's grasp, the electric fence controller would fire again, and the lightning bolt of electricity again used Jay's body as a shortcut to ground.

It seemed to go on forever. And with every new discharge cycle, Jay would spout yet another phrase of a language which I now believe must have been Ungulu—an obscure dialect spoken only in south-central Africa. It was hard for me to tell for sure, because of the high volume of saliva accompanying the shouted phrases.

That day, as the consummate huntin' buddy, Jay's actions saved me from the indignity of a botched half-crossing of that electrified fence. His sacrifice spared me from barbed wire scratches on my hands, arms, and legs. I didn't have the larger part of the crotch and one leg of my hunting pants ripped away. I didn't have electrical burns on the inside of my bare leg. I still had all the buttons on my shirt. I still had my hat. My eyesight remained clear and focused. I alone was able to continue to speak decent English, with good grammar, syntax, and pronunciation. And most of all, I didn't smell like fresh urine for the rest of the hunt.

But that's not where Jay's self-sacrifice ends. Jay also still displays a good sense of humor about the whole episode, as year after year I retell, with fastidious adherence to accuracy, the story of how it all unfolded. If a huntin' buddy does nothing else, he will certainly provide you with an unending flow of entertaining stories. I'm sure he enjoys the stories as much as I do telling them.

Oh, and this reminds me. Here's a helpful hint for those of you who want to be good huntin' buddies: In recent years, I have begun carrying a small white dry-erase board and marker in my backpack so when such circumstances present themselves (which now occur every time Jay and I go hunting), I can quickly hold up an appropriate score. If I had been thusly equipped that day, I would have scored Jay's Olympic-style gymnastics (combined with some moves only commonly seen in rodeo bull riding) as a 9.5, minimum. I firmly believe that Jay appreciates a high score when his self-sacrifice as a huntin' buddy is properly recognized.

Jay had searched his entire life for a *real* huntin' buddy, and ever since I came along, he has put considerable effort into keeping that relationship good. For my part of the relationship, I have been able to endure his good-hearted actions, and after applying deep layers of forgiveness, still enjoy going hunting with him.

So, fellow hunters, after years of carefully cultivating the relationship with your "huntin' buddy," please don't endanger it with careless acts. And if you do, be sure to find a huntin' buddy with a forgiving spirit.

In my experience, there are a number of common offenses one might commit against a huntin' buddy. So, as a service to the hunting community, I will now pass along some of my best hints, and even some sage advice, on how you might best preserve this hard-won relationship.

For ease of understanding, I will first set the stage for each common offense by a summary statement. Then I will offer a useful illustration in story form, set against the backdrop of an imaginary hunting trip that Jay and I might take to Colorado, in search of elk.

For lack of a more appropriate cast of characters (and not wishing to offend any innocent hunters out there whose names might coincidentally match those chosen here), I will simply cast Jay and myself in the parts of the "huntin' buddies" exemplified below.

Okay, so let's begin by setting the stage with some rudimentary facts regarding this "imaginary elk hunting excursion in Colorado" which will form the foundation of our illustrative scenarios.

Jay and I had been bowhunting for several days in early

September, high in the Rocky Mountains of central Colorado.

The first heavy snowfall had not yet come, and the elk were still very high. They were hanging out at night in the dark timber just below the tree line, and the big bulls were seen grazing on the forbs well above tree line.

For two days in a row, we rose early and hiked for hours to the tree line. We had seen distant elk, but didn't have time to get to them before it was time to head back to camp.

On day three of the hunt, Jay just didn't have the stamina to make that long climb once again. The short nights had taken their toll. He talked me into a hunt on the slopes adjacent to the highest place we could find to park the pickup. I reluctantly agreed. Predictably, all we saw was old elk sign.

As we ate our lunch from the tailgate of the parked pickup, I fought back the urge to remind Jay of the axiom, "hunt where the elk are." I then noticed something new. My abilities for predicting weather are far sharper than Jay's. What I saw in the sky was obvious. The brisk winds carrying low, gray clouds across the peaks from the northwest would soon bring snow.

It was not easy to talk Jay into making a dramatic change in our hunting tactics. I argued that we could pack up and climb that mountain now, to set up a spike camp for three days. That way we could sleep among the elk, preserve our strength, and dramatically extend the hunting day.

When I was finally able to talk Jay into another climb of that rugged mountainside, the sun was already on the decline. Even before the phrase, "Well ... okay" left his lips, I urged him to get moving and get packed. Even if we left immediately, we would likely finish the climb in the dark.

I pointed out to him the first sprinkles of rain in the darker stringers below the clouds at the crest of the mountain. Soon this would change to snow, I warned. I reminded Jay that we didn't want to try to climb this mountain in a snowstorm.

We had to get moving, and we had to get moving now. We had to gain another 800 feet of altitude up slopes that seemed vertical, and we wanted to complete the climb in daylight, if possible.

With these basic foundations laid for our imaginary hunting trip, we can continue with some illustrations of some things that in my imagination, perchance, might actually go wrong, and cause friction with a huntin' buddy. I have determined to call each offense a "sin," for that is by far the best descriptive term.

But before I continue with enumerating and illustrating each successive "sin," I want to take this opportunity to give the hunters of the world some sage advice on a few preliminary matters. Vigilance in these matters will pay dividends.

First helpful hint: Let's imagine that for some reason it becomes important to pack quickly for a long climb to establish a spike camp. In those circumstances, *never ever* let your huntin' buddy have unsupervised access to your backpack during the packing process. No matter how big or little your pack might be, all the really heavy stuff will somehow find its way into your pack.

If you don't believe me on this, just pick his bag up off the ground at the first rest stop. Make an excuse about looking at flowers or something so you can move his pack over to the left a foot or so without drawing suspicion. Be warned that when you lift his straps, you will almost hit yourself in the face with his bag from the unexpected differential in heft. But being a good huntin' buddy, it's best that you not blurt out something along the lines of, "Holy fried peaches! Are you carrying *anything* in your pack?"

And on top of that, following your inconvenient discovery of the truth, you should expect your huntin' buddy to deny the whole thing over and over, even attributing something weird once supposedly said by Davy Crockett about everybody else's pack seeming lighter.

Expect him to refuse your offer to trade packs so as to conclusively demonstrate that there isn't any real difference in the weights. Be ready for him to lamely excuse himself by saying something about not wanting to "take a chance on damaging" your far-better-than-his hunting gear.

When the rest break is over, expect him to step away briskly uphill, and then to push hard to stay well ahead of you from that point forward in the climb. The jovial conversations you had up to this point in the climb are now over.

Because his pack is demonstrably lighter, he will have no problem outdistancing you. The differential loading will allow him to set a pace that keeps you gasping for air, all the while poking fun at you any time you must rest and catch your breath. There is only so much oxygen saturation at this altitude, and he will be sucking down as much of it as he can—before you can get to it.

Second helpful hint: Let's assume in our imaginary trek that the long climb has reached the timber just below the tree line. It is absolutely essential that you catch up to your huntin' buddy well before he makes a unilateral decision on where to put the tent.

When you sense that he is looking left and right for a tent

site, then yell uphill to remind him to "find a level spot," you need to understand that your huntin' buddy might wrongfully interpret that instruction as finding a "flat spot." In his exhausted condition, he will forget that "flat" is a condition that can exist for a plane oriented at *any* angle. "Level," however, denotes a surface that is perpendicular to the pull of gravity. If your huntin' buddy isn't mechanically inclined, he won't appreciate this nuance.

Fellow hunters, if you don't intervene in time, you may find yourself in a tent whose floor slopes downhill so dramatically that everything you own (including your sleeping bag— containing your sleepless body) will soon be slumped into a pile against the downward margin of the tent.

Third helpful hint: If the tent is on a considerable slope, then never allow your huntin' buddy to orient the tent so its door is on the directly-downhill side of the tent. Trust me that some of the most important stuff you have in the tent—especially your only cans of stew—will easily roll down the floor, gaining sufficient momentum to push down the flimsy little door sill. Once free of any controls, they will bounce happily downward for a distance far greater than you will ever want to go to retrieve them.

Fourth helpful hint: Let's say you are securing the tent by pounding in the huge, heavy tent stakes— actually giant bridge nails with washers welded to the heads. Yep, those are the same heavy nails which your huntin' buddy cleverly hid within the six-man dome tent roll that *somehow* wound up in your pack. You don't actually mind pounding these into the ground because you really hate them, anyway. And if they never pull out of the ground ... that's okay by you.

As the first step in pounding the metal spike, you emplace

the tip of the huge nail through those cloth loops around the perimeter of the dome tent, and after pulling the floor inside the tent tight, you are about to hit it briskly with a big rock. It is at this juncture that things can go terribly wrong.

Fellow hunters, for the sake of all you hold dear, *never, ever, ever* slam that rock down on the head of that iron stake while your huntin' buddy is arranging his gear inside that tent.

Here's how it unfolds: It may not happen on the first stake, nor the next. But with one of those stakes, and at the time when the rock is at maximum acceleration downward toward the head of the nail, your huntin' buddy will do something inside that tent that unexpectedly jerks the floor about an inch. That event suddenly displaces the cloth loop which is firmly attached to that floor, also moving that nail's tip a similar distance. Your other hand grasps the big nail close to the bottom to keep tender fingers well clear of the impact zone. That's fine, but this hand also forms an effective fulcrum about which the nail freely and suddenly now rotates in the opposite direction.

In horror, your eyes and brain realize that the new impact point of the rock and the nail now includes the location of the fingers curling over the edge of the large rock. The brain immediately sends a "Stop!" signal to the extremities, but the speed of nerve conduction lags far behind the timing necessary to avoid an unacceptable outcome.

Your eyes will only be able to watch the remainder of the sequence in slow motion, as your brain quickly assembles a new vocabulary. Immediately following the fleshy "pthub" of the cushioned impact, you must drop everything and execute the traditional hop-dance in a random pattern in the vicinity of the camp, all the while fluently shouting random phrases in Ungulu.

Fifth helpful hint: Expect the unexpected. I have no idea how it happens, but on occasion, the strangest things happen in hunting camp. Some of them even defy the laws of nature.

Imagine with me, if you will, a hypothetical spike camp with a tent placed on an unreasonably steep slope, regardless of how flat it might be. Also imagine that the floor of this tent slopes so dramatically that your sleeping bag just barely has enough friction to stay on that floor without sliding downward to join the avalanche of other gear at the bottom of the tent—but only if you don't get in it and then change position. Every time you turn over, or even breathe deeply, you lose six inches. In no time at all, you find yourself at the bottom of the tent, among the sharp-edged stuff down there.

Imagine now that all you can do to regain your former sleeping location is to mimic a giant inchworm, using your free hands to grab handfuls of the tent floor so you can pull your knees up for another lurch. Imagine also that for some reason your sleeping bag does not want to cooperate *at all* in this repeating ritual, and on top of that it seems to be unnaturally heavy—especially at the top, under your rolled-up jacket, which substitutes for a pillow. All of this in your sleep-deprived state makes no sense to you at all.

So, you are left with few options upon awakening to find yourself for now the third time in the gear pile at the bottom of the tent. You do the mental math, and consider that a reasonable solution might be to simply remain part of the gear pile, with the off chance of getting any sleep at all before the coming dawn.

As you do the final calculation, the single dry pine needle holding your backpack in its position high above where your sleeping bag originally rested, finally fails with a faint "tick." That pack tumbles down, gaining momentum, and thuds to a rest across your chest. It goes no further. That's because it has expended all its considerable kinetic energy in its failed attempt to drive you and all the assembled gear through the lower wall of the tent. You believe you feel the nails you pounded in at the top of the tent give way slightly. These new variables now dramatically simplify the calculation, and you resolve to remain right where you are until dawn.

As dawn breaks, you get a chance to survey the tent for the first time in daylight. That's when you notice that there are deeper mysteries. For instance, how can it be that Jay's bag, although far slicker on the outside, still remains securely in its original location high on the tent's floor?

And *where in the world* did that huge, flat, sharp rock in my sleeping bag come from, which has been scraping me up all night long? It wasn't a bad dream after all.

Yep, some very strange things can happen in hunting camps.

So, with these helpful hints firmly in mind, let's now dive right into discussions of the various sins that a huntin' buddy might commit.

Sin: Not packing stuff you really need, but packing unnecessary stuff you don't need.

Example: Let's say that your huntin' buddy was in charge of packing all the food for the three days we'd spend at the spike camp. He'd planned a great menu. Our evening meal would be stew with crackers, washed down with some Earl Grey tea (sweetened with real sugar, of course). For breakfast, we would have eggs cooked to order with hash browns, and again the unmitigated joy of sweetened Earl Grey tea. Lunch in the woods on the hunt for elk would consist of trail mix and other high-energy snack foods.

Let's further say that since your pack was so completely chock-full of heavy camping gear, there was little room for food stocks. Since your huntin' buddy's pack was pretty much wide open, he had lots of room for all that food he'd promised.

So, what on earth could possibly explain why we would get to spike camp with only three cans of stew, a sack of cashews, some assorted Hershey treats, a pack of Fig Newtons, a box of Earl Grey tea, a large "army spoon," and a small camp stove with an assortment of aluminum pans? Note at this point that I packed the camp stove and the assortment of pans in *my own* backpack.

What you see missing in that list are some of the more important food items and utensils. Those would include eggs, potatoes, sugar, more cans of stew, some trail mix, a larger assortment of high-energy lunch items. How about a can opener to get into the stew cans? What would be wrong with a couple of tin cups to drink the Earl Grey tea? Maybe some crackers for the stew?

Since we had no eggs or hash browns, you can imagine why I was just a tad irritated when I discovered that I actually had, deep in my pack, a spatula, which I carried all the way up that mountain ... a totally useless, full-sized stainless-steel spatula, for crying out loud!

As we arose in the morning, I could only dream of fried eggs and hash browns. We had crunchy oatmeal bars instead.

The snow was still coming down lightly as we piled out of the tent after first light. We had come all this way to hunt ... and by golly, we were going to hunt!

The visibility was very poor in the fog and snow, and there were no bugles to be heard. We tried to hunt, but the increasing snow had the elk holed up and we weren't about to stumble over them. We threw up our hands and just decided to go back to the tent and cook up some dinner.

I recovered that odd flat rock that had sought comfort inside my sleeping bag, and with another rock under one end, I fashioned a safe spot to put the small camp stove. It provided some light, but more importantly, some needed heat.

We had to open the stew cans with knives, and began warming the meal on the stove. In the absence of crackers, Jay put a handful of cashews into the stew. After he'd seen me eyeing the spatula and shaking my head, Jay carefully deposited a single cashew half on its blade's corner, and tipped it so that the cashew piece fell into the stew. "There," he said as he held the spatula up in admiration. "I told you we'd need this."

We wiped out as much residual stew as we could from the cans, beat the sharp edges down as best we could, and sipped Earl Grey tea from them. Without sugar, we tried to dissolve small Hershey chocolate bars (laced with tiny peanut chips, because that was all we had) to sweeten the tea. I can tell you that the taste of lukewarm Earl Grey tea, laced with partially-dissolved chocolate, with more than a hint of bonus "stew flavor" is ... how shall I describe it ... *unusual*. I am confident that the Earl himself might have at that time spun in his grave. It might have been better if we didn't also have to sip it through gritted teeth to strain out all the little peanut particles.

I hoisted my sleeping bag to its original position again. There was a small "shelf" of sorts that was closer to level, where my backpack had been the first night, so I pulled my bag further up there for another try at slump-free sleep.

Overnight, I could hear Jay's muffled voice in his bag. He must be having great dreams of elk hunting, I surmised. I was to later find that his dreams were about an arctic walrus that kept rolling over on him. Those dreams were appropriate, since the foot of snow that fell overnight had collapsed the upper side of the tent, and he spent most of the night pinned between the collapsed tent and the floor.

For my part, I had the option of simply sliding back down to the bottom of the tent, where I slept like a baby, safe in a hammock.

As the faint light of dawn brushed the sky, Jay pushed and shoved the upper side of the tent to move enough snow away so he could have space to breathe. The clear skies brought with them a bitter cold, and we opted to just stay in the warm bags until the sun shone strongly. As I heard the zipper on Jay's sleeping bag slide to its full-up position, a huge bull elk bugled only a dozen yards away. Neither of us budged an inch.

Sin: Failing to come to a huntin' buddy's aid.

Now, in our imaginary hunting excursion, let's say that Jay and Bob tried to get into the mood to get out and hunt, but they were so hungry and tired, all they really wanted to do was to get back to the truck, and return to the warm trailer to cook some decent food ... and sip some unadulterated Earl Grey, hoping to paint over the part of their minds that clearly recollected the horrific aftertaste from the mixture they'd made the night before.

And so we began to strike camp. While doing that, the unexplained events were still happening. Somehow, an extra one of those huge homemade tent stakes showed up. And an unexplained small, perfectly round hole materialized in the upper part of the tent floor. I inquired about these, but Jay just shrugged his shoulders and kept packing. Fortunately, during a couple of minutes of unsupervised time with Jay's backpack, I was able to see that the big tent (and all the stakes, and even that spatula) would fit nicely in *his* pack. He was happy to find that out, I can tell you.

With our packs on our backs and bows in our hands, Jay and I started down the steep slopes to the pickup we could see parked in the bright sunshine bathing the deep valley below. Even as we descended to the mid-mountain level, there was a nice two-inch layer of fresh snow on the ground.

The events of the last two days had obscured, if not totally removed, the memory of those pesky slick-as-grease aspen leaves now hidden below the pristine snow (as invisible as land mines). Since we were in a hurry, we opted to just head straight through that aspen grove. Starvation and fatigue had wiped our memory-banks clean.

As Jay and I descended into the aspen groves, we failed to notice that there was a profound absence of any animal tracks. Looking back, that should have been our first clue. In the top of the grove, there are very few aspens, and they are all of small diameter. The steep slope didn't change all that much from when we came through this same grove on the way up. I estimated it to be only about five degrees steeper. As an odd turn of events, Jay hung back, and I found myself in the unusual position of leading the way.

Now, for our illustration, let's suppose that you are hanging onto a small aspen tree for dear life, just a dozen yards downhill from your huntin' buddy, when you hear something that sounds like "guff-swooooosh." As you turn to see what it is, he accelerates past you as if seated in an invisible bobsled. He reaches out toward you for help.

Alas, he passed by about a foot away, and I was only able to release my grip on the tree and reach a few inches to try to give him aid. After all, I still needed to maintain my firm grip on the tree so as to save him. Huntin' buddy etiquette does not require you to risk your own life in the aid of a huntin' buddy. I gave Jay a second chance by thrusting the heel of my boot quite briskly out at him as he went by.

Jay, now having squandered two opportunities to avoid the rest of what was to come, accelerated down the hill past me, leaving a wide groove in the snow, much like a bobsled run. He seemed to actually leave the ground a little as he disappeared over a low rise, with a cloud of snow and aspen leaves in the air behind him. The "swoooosh" terminated in a solid "thud," and the top of a small three-inch diameter aspen tree suddenly lurched a few yards downhill. The impact's sharp sound echoed off the far canyon wall.

Now, in our imaginary story, you, as a true huntin' buddy, intend to go down the hill, in total disregard to your own safety, to offer assistance. As you inch to the point where you can see down the steeper slope, you then discover that your huntin' buddy was able to cleverly arrest his rapid descent down the slope by using that lone aspen, which is still swaying gently. He was able to come to a safe stop by carefully guiding each of his legs to opposite sides of that tree, which is partially uprooted, and now leans downhill at about a 45 degree angle. Hmmm. I guess that's why they call them "quaking aspens." You learn a lot by spending time in the-out-of-doors.

The little aspen took a lot of stress as it heroically stopped your huntin' buddy, together with his hefty pack. Its odd angle relative to the slope will forever mark the location of where it saved the day. You now see that your huntin' buddy is lying fully back against his backpack, with both hands over his face. He is beginning to yodel, which you think somewhat odd, but still fits within the parameters of true alpine tradition. He is trying in vain to sit upright, and it's clear he needs your help.

Because time is of the essence in your desire to personally congratulate him on a clever way of stopping a high-speed descent, you determine that it will be best just to slide down the bobsled run yourself. You make that determination immediately following the time when both your feet slip completely out from under you, your death-grip on the thin aspen tree fails, and you find yourself speeding down the same bobsled run that Jay just carved in the powdery snow.

You are a true huntin' buddy. Self-sacrifice is your middle name. So it is that as you approach your huntin' buddy's resting place at an alarming (and increasing) rate of speed, you refuse to do what every other rational person would do—and that is to comfortably arrest your slide by placing a boot on either side of his shoulders.

Nope, you deftly roll over and negotiate the last 15 feet or so facedown, clawing at the hillside for any semblance of handhold. But the lack of any aspen trees prevents you from stopping as cleverly as your huntin' buddy did. Your congratulatory "slap on the back" will just have to wait. As you zip past your huntin' buddy, you notice that he's pushing you further off to the side. He is a true huntin' buddy, and he's clearly helping you maintain proper clearance from him as you pass.

At the last second, I saw that Jay moved his leg briskly toward me in an obvious attempt to give me the same "second chance" courtesy I had given him further up the slope. I gratefully accepted that bit of offered help, and wrapped both arms around Jay's leg. Using his boot like a substitute "tail hook," I jerked suddenly and safely to a halt. As I think back on it, the whole event bore a striking resemblance to a Navy fighter jet performing a carrier landing. I was impressed with my performance. I had just slowed from the speed of "oh-my-gosh!" to a complete stop in only a couple of inches. My momentum and dramatic increase of weight to his leg caused Jay to rotate only 20 or 30 degrees around the tree as I came to a halt in a short arc below him.

My clever use of the "carrier landing" technique also pleased and re-energized Jay, who sat briskly upright, his mouth and eyes wide open. He was considering thanking me for coming to his rescue, or possibly he was going to comment on my "tail-hook" technique, but he abandoned that effort, knowing it would just begin a long conversation about who was the better huntin' buddy, and all that. He and I didn't have time for that kind of extended adoration session; we needed to get to the truck.

So, Jay just flopped back down onto his back, and once again began yodeling, but this time at a much higher range.

That's okay. True huntin' buddies don't need all that kind of gushing emotionalism accompanying a good deed, or some inventive stopping techniques.

Because I am a true huntin' buddy, I won't tell Jay that this isn't the best time or place to practice yodeling. You don't have to tell your huntin' buddy everything, you know. What he doesn't know won't hurt him.

Somewhere in the distance, a pack of coyotes began to join in the song.

Good huntin' and good huntin' buddies.

ABOUT THE AUTHORS

Bob Baldwin

Bob Baldwin, an avid bow hunter since age 12, founded http://www.bowhuntinginfo.com/ in 1998, making it one of the earliest dedicated archery websites. Jay Ledbetter first contacted Bob through that website, and Bob and Jay soon became the best of "huntin' buddies."

Bob and Jay have hunted together for the last two decades, from Colorado to Michigan, and from the upper latitudes of Canada to Texas. It seems that during every hunting trip, something happens that leads to a story or two, and the occasional emergency-room visit.

The Bob 'n Jay stories of hunting and fishing adventures

began with Bob's love of telling humorous stories around hunting camp. Bob, never the one to embellish, would always tell the stories with fastidious adherence to accuracy, but it seemed that Jay would always retell them with a few of what Jay would always protest to be "minor adjustments."

Bob promises, "There is kernel of truth to all our stories. Some of the things that happen when hunting with good buddies just can't be made up, but any embellishments are solely the responsibility of Jay." The truth is that the funniest of the stories has the most truth.

Bob lives with his bride of 47 years, Shirley, in the state of Michigan, and Jay lives in Colorado. Many in the hunting community know well the constant flood of misadventures that plague Jay during his hunts. Predictably, these sad incidents invariably disrupt the peaceful and fulfilling hunts that Bob otherwise would enjoy. Observers all agree with Bob that it is wise for him to maintain a wide geographical separation from Jay for the majority of the year.

Jay Ledbetter

Jay Ledbetter began bow hunting as a young boy of 10, stalking across the prairie outside his little town in New Mexico. Jay used his cheap fiberglass recurve bow to propel heavy wooden arrows at speeds best measured with a calendar, toward any jack rabbit foolish enough to be within sight. No rabbits were harmed at any time, mind you, but many were mightily entertained by the aerial display.

Jay served his country in the U.S. Army (Infantry and SF), and was deployed a number of times overseas. Jay is fond of saying, "Only the Army can really mess up a camping trip!" Once Jay finished his time in the Army, he was able to dedicate more of his time to his love of hunting and fishing. And that's how he encountered Bob.

Bob helped Jay arrange for a television celebrity to hunt a rogue bison bull running wild on Jay's land, which was in danger of causing much damage, if not loss of life. The bison bull was also quite dangerous. From that time until today, Jay has identified Bob as his "huntin' buddy," and has been trying to get Bob to hunt with him every year for decades. As Bob's memory of the last preceding hunt with Jay begins to fade, Bob relents, and he and Jay head out once again to the woods. Thankfully, Bob has a short memory, because they go to the woods all the time.

Jay's succession of pratfalls and other hunting calamities has provided Bob with an endless series of true stories to tell, which have become the genesis of the Bob 'n Jay adventure series of books. So, as Bob admits, the hunting trips with Jay "haven't been a total loss."

Jay resides in Colorado with Denise, his bride of 39 years.

www.ingramcontent.com/pod-product-compliance
Lightning Source LLC
Chambersburg PA
CBHW071151090426
42736CB00012B/2300